living with light

living with light

decorating the Scandinavian way

gail abbott

photography by **mark scott**

CICO BOOKS

LONDON NEW YORK

For May and James

Published in 2008 by CICO Books
an imprint of Ryland Peters & Small
519 Broadway, 5th floor, New York, NY 10012

www.cicobooks.co.uk

10 9 8 7 6 5 4 3 2 1

A CIP catalog record for this book is available from the
Library of Congress.

ISBN-13: 978 1 906094 32 4
ISBN-10: 1 906094 32 2

Printed in China

Editor: Gillian Haslam
Designer: Christine Wood
Photographer: Mark Scott

contents

introduction

In the far northern countries of Scandinavia, the clear summer light is one of the dominant features of the landscape. Forests, seas, lakes, and mountains are bathed in its clarity, and for half the year the sun hardly sets below the horizon. The people make the most of the outdoors while they can, for the winter means long, dark days in which the light is low and short-lived. Because of this, light is a quality that is highly valued.

In their homes, the Scandinavians make every effort to maximize any gleam of light that enters. Simple, clutter-free rooms painted white have bleached floors and understated window dressings. This design element has its roots in the eighteenth century, when the designers of the Swedish court were influenced by the neo-classical tastes of the more flamboyant French style. This was tempered and simplified, resulting in a restraint that combined pale floors and understated curtains with ornate, gilded furniture.

The style we know today as Gustavian Provincial Style, with its color palette of soft white, pale grays, and blues, evolved as the designs were simplified and developed for country parsonages and town houses. In the late nineteenth century, the artist Carl Larsson and his textile designer wife, Karin, published a book of Carl's paintings of their family home at Sundborn. The pictures showed

simple rooms decorated with painted furniture and woven textiles, and had a huge impact on Scandinavian interiors which continues to inspire interior design today.

These elements are easily put together to create an interior style that is simple and unassuming, and whether you live in a city apartment or a country house, clutter-free rooms and a pale color palette are a flawless formula that will help achieve a look that is filled with light. Many of the houses in this book are family homes, and the essentially practical nature of washable floors and removable slip covers make the rooms easy to live in, too. Learn how to use every surface to

reflect light into small rooms using mirrors and gleaming materials like stainless steel and chrome, and discover the way that accent color can lift a white room and help bring the outside in.

The houses range from a new seaside house on the Stockholm archipelago to a tiny studio in London, from a farmhouse near the Arctic Circle to an English country cottage—all very different locations and living situations. But every room has as its underlying principle that of allowing in as much light as possible. It's a way of living that stays close to nature and the cycle of the seasons in true Scandinavian style.

left: The simplicity of this dining room, with its white walls and gauzy muslin curtains, is underlined by the single blue-and-white plate used for display and the understated country flowers. The traditionally-inspired dining chairs, with their checked linen seat covers, are Gustavian in style.

right: Built into an uncurtained bay window that overlooks the sea, a white-painted wooden bench seat has been designed as a place to linger and enjoy the view whatever the weather. On the pale floorboards lies a hand-woven rag rug in muted colors that has been handed down through the generations.

light on white

White walls, sheer white muslin at the windows and white floorboards, this is the essence of an interior style that is seen throughout many homes in Scandinavia. It's a look that has evolved to make the most of every bit of available light.

left: A floor-length muslin curtain is wafted by the breeze on a hot day. Long windows are left open in summer, and in winter allow as much light in as possible.

right: Surrounded by summer homes built at the turn of last century, in the living room of this new house on the Stockholm archipelego, the fireplace pays tribute to the traditional ovens to be found across the island.

living with white

The essential ingredients of the all-white living room can be adapted for a new house just as successfully as for one that is traditionally-built. The materials and finish might be slicker, the spaces open plan and the furniture contemporary in style, but the overall elements remain the same. During the cold, dark Scandinavian winters, a reliable source of heat over and above the background underfloor heating is essential if the white walls are not to feel cold and unwelcoming. The result is that the wood-burning stove has been developed to a fine art. An effective modern stove can be fitted into a contemporary room, bringing with it an element of tradition to the pared-down interior. Double- or even triple-glazed windows are indispensable if gauzy curtains, clipped up to filter summer sunlight, are to be left in place throughout the winter months.

above: A modern sofa and armchair, covered in washable, white linen slip covers, update the Gustavian-inspired sitting room and makes it comfortable enough for the family to watch television. The new clock has been painted to look old, and is a witty touch that gives the room a focal point.

above right: An antique glass ceiling lamp has a clever "rise and fall" mechanism, with a counterbalance weight, that allows it to be pulled down over the table in the evenings.

right: If you are not artistically inclined, make simple panels by fitting strips of decorative beading with mitered corners to a plain wall and painting them to match. It's a simple device that quickly gives a Gustavian feel to any room.

Just outside Skellefteo, in the far north of Sweden, the owners of this country farmhouse found an empty house that had been unlived in for two years. With the help of a talented artist, they have brought a breath of fresh air to all the rooms with wit and a light touch. Taking their inspiration from the delicacy of the Gustavian era, softly painted wall panels and rococo swags give the sitting room a look of gently fading elegance that has the feel of a much grander house about it. Throughout this region of the country too, many farmhouses dating from the seventeenth century onward had colorful stenciled or hand-painted decorations on the walls, often in the form of painted canvas panels that were hung only for festival days. This tradition lives on in the painted decorations throughout the house.

Above the windows, simple wooden pelmets hide the metal curtain poles, to which floor-length muslin curtains are clipped, making it just a moment's work to take them down for washing. In the pure air of northern Sweden, white curtains stay white for a long time, but any city dweller knows how often a pair of white curtains will need changing, and clipping up sheers saves time as well as expensive dry-cleaning bills.

Against the antiqued and decorated walls, a combination of comfortable upholstered furniture and a modern glass coffee table stop the room looking like a museum piece—a look that can be just as effective whether you live in a city apartment or a country house.

above: The floor is carpeted to keep out cold drafts that would otherwise come up through the uninsulated floorboards. The curtains are thick and padded at the single-glazed windows, and an open log fire roars in the traditional hearth.

left: A handful of late-summer garden flowers— anemone japonica and white marguerites—are augmented with boughs of silver pear and twigs of pussy willows collected in the spring.

An old country house in Dorset, England, takes all the fundamentals of the Scandinavian style—white walls and ceiling, white-covered sofas and a pale floor that work together to make any room appear bigger than it actually is—but in a happy marriage of style influences, the owners have also brought traditional British elements to their living room.

white heat

In the oldest Swedish houses, the fireplace was always placed in the corner of the room. When the tiled stoves of the eighteenth century replaced the traditional open hearth, they took the same position. The highly-efficient design of these stoves means that just one or two logs in the small firebox heat the stove's brick interior for hours. The heat is stored and given out slowly throughout the day, much like a modern storage heater.

above left: Tiled stoves were an expensive luxury, but even a maid needed a heated bedroom in the far north of Sweden, which can have snow for five months of the year. This pretty stove in a child's bedroom has been restored to its former state, which was not tiled but rendered in cement for economy.

above: Divided into squares and given a delicate motif by a modern artist, the cement surface is decorated with hand-painted "faux" tiles.

Many of the most beautiful tiled stoves were manufactured at the Gustavsberg porcelain factory near Stockholm, which first opened in 1826. With a breathtaking range of different colors and designs to be found on the tiled exteriors, these elegant yet hard-working stoves graced some of the most beautiful royal palaces, such as Gripsholm, the winter quarters of King Gustaf III, as well as the homes of the wealthy middle classes.

above left: A white-tiled stove is only one of many in this Swedish house that was built in 1887. Each room has its own corner stove, and in deepest winter the house is as warm as if it had state-of-the-art central heating.

above: The white porcelain detailing around the base and top of the stove gives it a refined charm. Antique stoves are readily available, but need a skilled fitter to put them together.

window style

Covered with thick forests of beech, birch and pine, it is wood that has always been the major building material in Scandinavia. Most houses even today are constructed with heavy-duty insulation material and clad with weatherboard planks that are painted to protect them from the elements. Inside, many of the older properties are wood paneled, from the elegant eighteenth-century rooms of the neo-classical era, to the simpler tongue-and-groove ceilings of more modest homes. The architects of the summer homes built on the islands near Stockholm were no exception, and some of the detailing has a lightness of touch that can only be achieved with wood.

Until the end of the nineteenth century the islands of the Stockholm archipelago—some 30,000 small islands scattered north, east and south of the city—had been home to only the hardiest fishermen and farmers when they were discovered as a vacation destination by artists and writers, such as August Strindberg. When the bourgeoisie of Stockholm began to appreciate their wild beauty, there was a rush to build summer homes where the families of the merchant classes could enjoy the short summer, with its long, light days over the Baltic.

Today, many of the inhabitants of Stockholm, whose main home is usually an apartment in the city, have a cottage on an island, where most spend their summer vacations. Some of the closer islands are only a half an hour's travel from the city center, so some of the turn-of-the-century homes are lived in all year round. With tongue-and-groove-clad walls and ceilings and intricate windows letting in light wherever there was an opportunity to put one, the all-white interiors show a fascinating range of design and detail.

above left: Sneaked into the eaves of this island family home, a small arched window lets light into the top of the stairs. Curved glazing bars give it a look of a church window and add to the decorative effect. Sitting on a tiny ledge below the window, a small model boat illustrates the family's love of sailing.

left: With its set of curved windows in the entrance hall letting in light on three sides, this holiday home belongs to a Swedish family living in London. Making the most of their time on the island, they play, swim, water-ski, and eat outside whenever possible.

right: A French armoire has found its way into the entrance hall of the summer house. Its intricately-carved finial and beveled mirrors give a touch of grandeur to the room, but one that is well matched by the curve of the windows and the depth of the architraves.

above: Simple windows need only the simplest curtain treatment, and a pair of sheer, tab-top curtains do very little but filter the light as it streams through a kitchen window. A small red berry heart adds a flash of color and is a typically Swedish decoration.

above right: In traditionally-built Swedish houses, the windows have a second, internal window that acts as deep secondary glazing, keeping rooms warm through the long winters.

left: The windows of an all-white dining room stand serenely in the summer light. In this northern home, the sun stays high until almost midnight in June and July, and the inhabitants testify to plenty of warm, sunny weather. This is some compensation for the months of darkness, they say, when the sun hardly appears above the horizon. Heavy curtains would block out the precious light, so a mere wisp of muslin is all that's required, even in winter.

bath house

One of the Scandinavian's major obsessions is with the sauna. The health benefits of raising the body temperature and expelling toxins are well known, and many people round off their sauna experience with a dive into cold water, or even a dip though an ice hole. The coastline is sprinkled with tiny wooden huts perched on rocks, and the owners of this house on the river have built their own sauna and "bath house" on the riverbank, where they can entertain friends and relax afterward.

left: A salvaged metal-framed window has been let into the wall of the wooden bath house and, with no neighbors nearby, the window has been left uncurtained. A small wood-burning stove heats the room, which has been comfortably furnished with rattan chairs and a padded bench.

right: The wooden bench seat is topped with deep mattress pillows in white linen, and heaped with textured white pillows and small duvets for extra warmth in winter. A painted wooden stool acts as a coffee table, for wine glasses and snacks.

outdoor whites

Outside light can be reflected in the garden, as in the house, with the use of white. A painted fence will throw light back into a small space and a bank of simple white flowers is guaranteed to lift your spirits. At night, a "moon garden," planted with white flowers, such as cosmos, "Iceberg" roses, white peonies, and nicotiana, will maximize the silvery light, and its luminosity will make a night-time stroll an appreciated indulgence.

right: On a bright, summer's morning, the pure white of ox-eye daisies drifts through meadows and roadside verges and are often to be found in the Swedish garden.

below: A low picket fence has been treated with a white stain. Its decorative shapes serve to enhance the boundary of the garden, especially when flowers are allowed to self-seed through it.

small kitchens

Reflective white is a favorite kitchen choice for many cooks in Scandinavia, and when a kitchen is compact, it seems obvious to make the most of every bit of light. With so many kitchen options available these days, this can mean anything from contemporary high-gloss units to a set of white-painted tongue-and-groove doors. Designing a small kitchen takes careful planning, and if space is limited, clever storage solutions need to be utilized if the area is not to look overcrowded and cluttered. Units with "magic corners" that store cookware in hard-to-reach cabinets are fantastic and it might be necessary to find alternative places for the washing machine and tumble dryer. A cupboard under the stairs or a corner of the bathroom can be viable alternatives for these.

The choice of materials helps to determine the overall feel of the kitchen—stainless steel used for worktops, sink, and splashbacks bounces the smallest glimmer of light back into the room and gives the kitchen a professional feel, whereas a wooden worktop made from beech will warm up an all-white scheme and gives the kitchen a much more homely, country look.

left: In this tiny London kitchen, much thought has been given to every aspect of storage. The hanging rack above the sink holds pots and pans that would otherwise have to be stored in cabinets.

above right: The glossy white wall units have folding doors that open out to make the corners more easily accessible.

right: The original 1920s, steel Crittal windows in the kitchen have slender glazing bars that let in as much light as possible.

right: In this tiny utility room in a country house, a tall broom cupboard has been designed to store the vacuum cleaner, ironing board, and brooms neatly out of sight. The simple painted wood and black iron door latch make for a homely, vintage feel. The Belfast ceramic sink is deep enough to wash muddy boots, and also comes in useful for arranging cut flowers brought in from the garden.

above: This small painted kitchen, inspired by Swedish interiors, was built using medium density fiberboard, and scored to look like tongue-and-groove wooden boards. The shelf under the wall cupboard is a clever way to introduce a little more storage space and provides a pretty display area for a pair of French enamel jars.

right: A small kitchen table gets a touch of class when it's laid with a few choice pieces. The pure white cloth, decorative white china, sparkling glassware and silver flatware will glint in the light, whether it's sun streaming through the window or candlelight at night.

family kitchens

Modern kitchens the world over often have to perform a double function in a family home; they need to be efficient and practical places where food is stored, prepared, and cooked, and at the same time act as a versatile place where family and friends can get together. As well as acting as an everyday dining area, the kitchen table will often be a place to chop vegetables, talk to friends, and where the children congregate to do their schoolwork. The latest materials and designs can be teamed successfully with traditional elements, especially if they are all in white, and will help a multi-functional kitchen feel welcoming and a place to linger.

In this family-sized kitchen in a Swedish seaside home, the owners did their research and managed to find an antique cast-iron stove very much like the one that would have been part of the original kitchen. The wood store and brick hood above the stove were faithfully reproduced, but the rest of the kitchen was built with an eye to efficiency and hygiene. The bright white metro-style tiles around the cooking area and sink, and the modern fitted units stay spotlessly clean with the minimum of effort, and the tongue-and-groove paneling has been painted in easy-to-clean white gloss.

left: A twenty-first-century electric glass hob sits next to the antique wood oven which is lit in winter for warmth, and the wooden table has been stained and sealed for everyday use.

left: On a staircase with no external window, it can be necessary to light stairs artificially. Rather than use wall lights, discreet floor-level lights will throw light across the treads and on to a facing wall.

right: In this newly-designed home, the upper floor is clad in white-stained wood throughout. The narrow gallery under the eaves leads from the master bedroom to a small, sunny home office.

white on wood

In a country where wood is the preferred material and letting in light is the biggest concern, constructing a new home from wood seems the obvious choice for many people in Scandinavia looking to build. In many of the older houses, especially those built at the turn of the last century, all wood is painted, but a more contemporary alternative for internal spaces is to use a white wood stain. This looks fresh and modern, allowing the grain of the wood to show through but still reflecting light throughout. It's a practical solution, too, for high ceilings and lofty spaces, as planks can be stained before being put in place, and will need no attention for many years.

Bare wooden floorboards are practical in any house, whether old or new, but in an old house, they can prove drafty unless the gaps between are filled. As older boards can be a bit battered, they usually look best if sealed with a clear varnish, so letting the natural color through and minimizing the imperfections. They can be successfully painted with white or pale gray floor paint, too. When floorboards are laid on top of insulation and the wood is new, giving them a bleached look makes a floor that is pale and light-reflecting, warm to bare feet, and easy to clean. Modern alternatives are low-cost laminates, wood veneers, or a real wood floor that can be laid on top of floorboards or concrete.

above: All the bare bones of this new-build house are left exposed. The beams and wooden ceiling have been stained white, and suspended pendant lights made of aluminium add a nautical air.

left: In Scandinavia, bare wooden floorboards are often treated with a few coats of white oil, or even a solution of lye which bleaches the color out of the wood. The floors are regularly cleaned with proprietary white soap diluted in warm water, which builds up color over the years and forms a hard-wearing finish.

letting in the light

The nineteenth-century architect who designed this Swedish island house lost no opportunity to design windows wherever he could fit them. On a narrow flight of stairs leading up to two attic bedrooms, a circular window has been let in to the external wall and another half window squeezed in further up. It seems a quirky and delightful touch to us, but before the time of electric lighting, this stairway would have been dark and difficult to maneuver without any natural light, so the addition of these two little windows has a strictly practical function. As the house was only ever used in summertime, when there is plenty of light until almost midnight, the stairs are guaranteed to be well lit at all times and the round windows are an elegant and witty solution to a perennial lighting problem.

To reflect the small amount of light that is let in through the windows, and helping to double its effect, all the walls and woodwork on the stairs and landing are painted in white. The floorboards throughout the house have been sealed with a clear varnish so that the natural color of the wood comes through, and this gives a warm glow to all the rooms. The treads of the stairs have a similar finish, but each riser has been painted white. This gives a two-tone effect that makes it easier to keep your footing when going upstairs, and the matte finish to the varnish helps eliminate slipping.

above left: At the top of the stairs, the landing is well illuminated by a pair of tall arched windows and the delicate cross bars of the banisters allow in even more sunshine.

left: The round window on the stairs brings a maritime air to the house, with its echo of the porthole windows on the steam boats that would once have carried the family to their summer dwelling.

right: Seen from the outside of the house, the window which is cut in half by the stairs is a complete circle, so the symmetry of the design is complete. The small piece of baseboard stops small objects rolling off the stairs.

the white bedroom

Window treatments have many different functions and while in Scandinavia they are used for softening a plain window or filtering light, in countries where privacy is important, sheer white curtains or a voile shade can be a discreet way to maintain seclusion without losing light, especially in a city environment. If you like a dark bedroom at night, a blackout roller shade fitted behind the sheers is a simple way to provide this without losing the effect of the transparent fabric by day. There are plenty of alternatives to old-fashioned net curtains and furnishing fabric shops will have a wide range to choose from. You can locate materials like white butter muslin, cotton lawn and fine veiling in dress fabric shops too, to be made into unstructured shades and unlined curtains. Search out unusual textiles, like organza, taffeta, and tulle, for glamorous effects which will shimmer as they catch the light.

Sheer fabrics at the window can have the added bonus of shading a room from the dazzling effects of strong sunlight in a south-facing room, protecting valuable furniture and fabrics from fading. The beauty of many sheer fabrics is that they are inexpensive so can be used in abundance. In a very sunny room, the fabric will be affected by sunlight, and will eventually start to rot, so choosing a budget-priced fabric needn't break the bank when it is time to replace it.

above: Hung from a narrow metal curtain pole, a set of floor-to-ceiling curtains serve as a wall of fabric when they are drawn across the window. Simple curtains like these need only a gathered heading tape stitched across the top and they are ready to hang.

right: The abundant folds of sheer muslin curtains shield an indoor garden from the burning rays of the July sun. The contrast of textures between agapanthus petals and the curtain behind makes a beautiful focal point in an all-white bedroom.

above: An understated paint effect gives a hint of subtle texture to a modern chest of drawers. The effect is of a vintage piece, and the French enamelware jug and tureen have the slightly distressed look that only comes from years of use.

left: White on white makes this bedroom in a Victorian terraced house in London appear bigger than it really is. Built-in cabinets in the alcoves keep books behind glass and the mirror reflects filtered light from the windows.

above: A small mirror is placed in an unusual position behind a bedside cabinet, but facing it is a small round window from which daylight is bounced back under the white-painted eaves.

right: This attic bedroom would seem shadowy and dark if it wasn't for the layering of whites on all the surfaces. The king-size bed is pushed right up to windows dressed with uncomplicated Roman shades.

white in the bathroom

While practicality has to be the most important factor in any bathroom, making a room that combines highly functional features with beautiful design can be a challenge. Using white is a typically Scandinavian way of creating a bathroom sanctuary that is both feasibly practical and soothingly relaxing, but without careful use of texture, an all-white bathroom can look cold and clinical. The unrelieved shine of ceramic wall tiles and white fittings can create a room that is efficient and serviceable, but is the last place to linger.

The judicious combination of textures and materials within an all-white bathroom can serve to enhance even the smallest space. Simple painted paneling will give a surface that breaks up reflected light. Salvaged white marble will add natural texture when fitted around a white basin, and plain floor tiles can be laid in a diagonal pattern that appears to push the space outward. Even inexpensive white ceramic tiles can be given a more interesting texture if fitted in a brick-work design instead of the standard repeat. Fitting a row or two of more expensive mosaics as a border will bring interest to a plain, tiled splashback.

left: The high ceiling of this attic bathroom could have resulted in a room that looks out of proportion, but the black and white diagonal floor tiles and border paneling bring solidity to the lower part of the room. The enameled, cast-iron bath tub stands in the middle of the room and echoes the shape of the high, arched windows.

above: A pretty, country-style bathroom has been put into a room that was conceived as a bedroom when this Victorian house was built. The tongue-and-groove walls and bare floorboards are painted white, and the wooden storage unit houses baskets for towels, as well as a round basin plumbed in beneath the wooden top.

left: A Plexiglas splashback has been printed with an under-sea design in gold behind the bath tub in this children's bathroom. It's an amusing and eye-catching alternative to standard tiling and makes the most of contemporary materials.

below: The unusual shape of this bathroom depends on clever use of space. A walk-in shower is hidden behind a mosaic-tiled screen, but the wall is pierced with a small storage shelf that breaks up the expanse of tiling.

right: The mosaic-tiled walls and floor, white ceramic fittings and the sharp-edged mirror in this bathroom are considerably softened and muted by a muslin panel that is caught up on hooks at the window.

color accents

Pale walls and white surfaces give an authentic Swedish feel to a room, but the use of an accent color at the window will add individuality and interest. The restrained use of fabric and color that has come to be associated with Swedish style today began with Gustavian interiors, especially those manor houses, parsonages, and town houses of the middle classes which made use of simple fabrics for drapery. The artist Carl Larsson, whose family home at Sundborn in Sweden was the subject of many of his paintings, was another huge influence, and striped fabrics are often seen in the simple and elegant rooms he portrayed.

A country woven stripe, in natural fabrics like cotton and linen, makes the most unpretentious shades for a kitchen, shielding the room from strong sunlight but injecting a welcome glow of color. Heavy linings and interlinings are unknown in most Scandinavian homes and using unlined fabrics for curtains and shades will make sure that maximum light is allowed in.

Simple striped fabrics are widely available. Look for French mattress ticking which you can find in a wide range of colors, from red and blue, to green, pink, and even yellow. Ticking is particularly useful for roller shades as it has an inherent stiffness of fabric which helps it pull up evenly, but the exact color is not as important as the unassuming nature of the fabric.

left: A large kitchen has space for two tables, one for food preparation and one for eating. The red-and-white ticking shades over the windows contrast with the blue glass lampshades that are suspended over each working area. Blue ceramics and a vase of country flowers add color accents to the bright, white room.

One of the most typically-Swedish window treatments is the roll-up shade. It is one of the easiest shadess to make, involving no elaborate threading system and needing no battens, apart from one at the top that is attached to the window frame. A wooden dowel fed through the bottom hem helps the shade to roll up and a white nylon cord passes under the dowel and through simple glass rings stitched to the front of the shade. It's a modest system, but one that gives any window a quick and efficient, fuss-free covering. Used in a living room, a pair of muslin curtains would frame a similar shade and soften the overall effect.

above left: A garden gate in a Swedish village is painted a modest white, but a splash of vivid color has been introduced on the adjoining fence and mailbox, and by the purple lupins that grow wild all over the country.

above: Made from red-and-white-striped ticking, a pair of Swedish roll-up shades are fixed to the top of a white-painted window. The shades can be let down so that their color is seen to full advantage, or pulled high up so they are out of sight.

right: The woodwork on this custom-made storage unit is painted brilliant white, while the glass cupboard fronts reflect the red and white fabric of the shades. The tiny blue metal chair, used as a decorative accessory, is a typical Swedish design.

In nature, strong color accents throw into relief the whiteness of the landscape during the long Scandinavian winters. A cluster of bright red berries seen in a hedgerow, a dark green pine tree silhouetted against a white hillside, or the rich color of an unexpectedly clear blue sky above snow-covered farmland—all stand out brilliantly against a white backdrop. Inside too, a strong dash of color will balance the dazzling effect of a white room. The natural grain of bleached wood, the glinting highlights of a reflective kitchen unit, or the matt snowiness of a painted wall are all thrown into relief by the bold introduction of color. Red and blue are characteristic colours but any vivid tones, used with restraint, will inject a touch of drama.

left: A typical fabric, and one that will immediately say "Swedish" when it's introduced into a white room, is red-and-white woven check. It's a pattern that has all the freshness and simplicity of Gustavian style.

right: Decorated with gold scrolls on a deep blue background, this modern fabric recalls the ormolu decorative furniture of eighteenth-century grand houses and adds elegance and color to a contemporary interior.

mixing patterns

As well as stripes and checks, the originators of Swedish style often used unassuming floral fabrics for everything from bed drapes to wall coverings. These emulated the more extravagant embroidered silks of the French court, but like everything else Scandinavian, were used in a restrained and simplified way. The fabrics seen most often were modest sprigged florals printed in one color, and were usually used unlined. These fabrics were so simple that the same one could be used on curtains, bed drapes, and bed covers without looking too fussy, but this look relied on the remainder of the room being

above left: The wallpaper in this Swedish dining room is a muted white floral pattern printed onto a neutral background. This gives the room a subtly traditional feel, although the design is a contemporary one.

left: Midsummer is always a time for celebration throughout Sweden, when a red and white cake made with strawberries and cream is traditionally served.

right: Three patterns have been used together here—a subtly woven chair fabric, a red and green floral pillow, and a footstool in red, white, and natural stripes. It's the controlled color palette that makes this combination look so harmonious.

uncluttered and light, with bare floorboards, pale walls, and a chair or two covered in an unpretentious check.

Teaming different patterns in the same room relies on using a restrained color palette if the overall effect is not to be overwhelming and fussy, and you can bring the best of this traditional look to a modern room by following simple principles. Use pale, natural-colored or white linen for upholstered furniture like chairs and sofas, add a flash of color with a floral pillow or two, and include some bold stripes or a checked fabric for contrast.

below: In this dining room, red-and-white striped fabric has been used for the dining chair covers. It's a bold statement, but the lightness of the room, with its large amount of window, translucent white muslin shades and limed floor, gives the room a bright, welcoming feel.

east-coast chic

The sea and boats are very close to the heart of the many Scandinavian people who sail or motor out to their seaside homes, and summer living often means that nautical style comes inside. Red, white, and blue is a favorite color combination for interiors, and when it's given a maritime flavor it is a look that is immediately recognized as contemporary seashore style.

Walk along the narrow streets of a Swedish seaside town with its picturesque, painted weatherboard houses, and you'll notice that almost every house has a model sailing vessel displayed in one window, leaving you in no doubt that you are by the sea. Each house also has its own flagpole, and it's a rare family that doesn't hoist the Swedish flag every morning in summer. This style is often found along the eastern seaboard of America too—a reminder that the Swedish and Americans share a common heritage from the time of the first European settlers. Bright and breezy, east-coast style has a tang of salt that's difficult to resist.

left: If you love the sea, recreate the look in moments against the perennial backdrop of white painted walls, white linen sofa covers, and sheer muslin curtains. Just add a set of red- and blue-striped pillows and a model boat and the look is yours.

above right: A vintage wooden armchair has been re-upholstered in cotton fabric in a seaside bathroom. With a minimum of work, the chair has been given a new lease of life and brings a flash of color to a monochrome room.

right: This cotton fabric is printed with colorful naval ensigns in red, blue, and gold. It's a popular fabric in many island homes and reflects Sweden's seafaring history.

left: White-painted bookshelves take up the whole of one wall in this London apartment. The large collection of art books is cataloged by subject, and the resulting patchwork of color makes the room look lived-in and friendly.

right: These days, most homes require a desk space, and whether you work from home or just need somewhere to pay bills, a dedicated area where you can quietly perform these tasks is necessary. This tiny conservatory under the eaves makes a peaceful sanctuary away from family life for a garden designer. The bright red pillow on the chair adds a welcome touch of color.

homework

Storage is one of the most important considerations when it comes to designing a room, and only when a sensible and practical system has been designed and built can other elements of the room be planned. If your aim is for an uncluttered, white living room, a large collection of books may seem a distraction, but a room is also for living in. A well-designed shelf unit with closed cabinets underneath is one of the best ways of solving this problem and colorful rows of books on display will certainly bring a little riotous, if contained, color into the room. One way of bringing order to chaos is to sort books into color blocks rather than by subject. Low-level cabinets can bring all other storage needs together, and leave the rest of the room clutter-free.

monochrome and silver

For color to make an impact, it doesn't necessarily have to be vivid and bold. The discreet tones of black with an accent of silver will add depth to white, especially in winter. Where white reflects every bit of light and black absorbs and holds it, the sheen of silver softly echoes the qualities of both. The intrinsic qualities of silver and black in a white room make them ideal partners for a Christmas table. Start with a white tablecloth as the foundation and add a narrow length of black and white fabric down the center as a table runner. Set the table using pure white china, sparkling silver flatware and candlesticks, and plenty of gleaming wine glasses. With silver-sprayed plant pots in the center to hold trailing ivy and a pair of glass bowls containing silver Christmas baubles, it's a contemporary look far removed from the traditional red and gold, and one that will complement any modern dining room.

above: Three glass pendant lights are fixed so that they focus pools of light along the length of the table. Combined with the glow of candlelight, the lights provide a cozy radiance in the evenings.

left: This table set in a contemporary dining room is laid for a summer evening party, but with its black-and-white runner, silver plant holders and green foliage, it would work just as well for a festive meal in winter.

summer blues

Disarmingly simple, blue and white are as fresh and easy to live with as a summer's day. In countries where the warm months are short, homeowners like to make the interiors of their house as delightful as a walk outside, and there's nothing quite like the combination of sky blue and brilliant white to evoke the wide-open spaces of the Scandinavian countryside. As blue is a naturally "receding" color, it is guaranteed to make a room look bigger. The particularly soft shade known as "Gustavian Gray" makes a good link between the two, and the blend of white walls, gray paintwork, and blue gingham in this country breakfast room gives a feel of lightness and airiness that is unsurpassed by any more sophisticated color scheme. The classic bench seat under the window holds up to four people, and is a characteristic seating arrangement in Swedish kitchens.

left: This gray, drop-leaf breakfast table is decorated with a pair of candlesticks and a vase of deliciously overblown white peonies. The double pendant light throws pools of light onto the table beneath on dark mornings.

above right: An antique wall-mounted plate rack is original to this turn-of-the-century house. Its battered paintwork, blue underneath a top coat of white, links it with the traditional blue and white plates on display.

right center: Scandinavian food is traditionally healthy and simple, and this very thin flat bread, baked without yeast, sugar, or fat, is typical of a northern breakfast, often topped with hard cheeses or cold meat.

below right: Vintage wooden dining chairs, painted in Gustavian Gray, have the straight-backed slats that distinguish this most characteristic of furniture design.

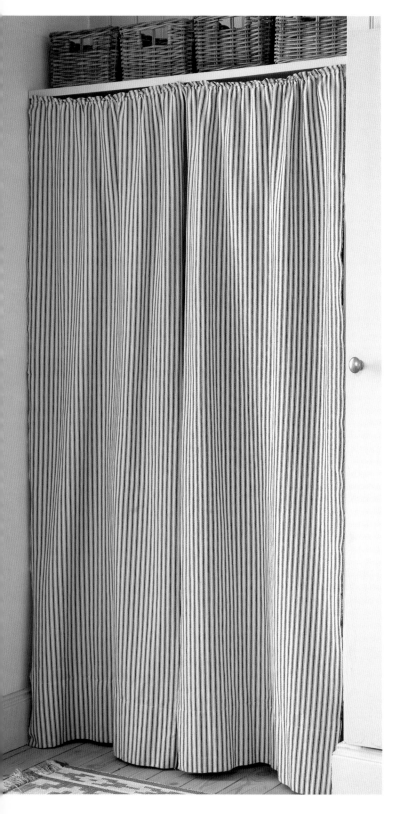

simply gray

In a typically unadorned hallway, pale gray paintwork on all the woodwork unifies the curve of the staircase with the storage units below. Scandinavian stairs are rarely carpeted and the wood is often left bare and sealed with a natural varnish or oil. Painting both risers and treads to match the surrounding baseboards will make a narrow set of stairs look much wider. To get a similar effect yourself, sand back the wood after stripping it of any old varnish or paint, trying to leave it as smooth as possible as any imperfections will be obvious when painted. Use two or three coats of good-quality floor paint on stairs, as they will get a great deal of wear, and the same paint can be used on the surrounding woodwork. Leaving outdoor shoes at the door is a very sensible custom that is followed on entering any Scandinavian house, and helps keep the floors and stairs clean and un-scuffed.

left: A wooden shelf holds baskets used for gloves, scarves, and hats in the hall. A blue-and-white striped curtain is strung on wires and makes a low-cost coat closet that is beautifully simple.

right: Added to the structure of the stairs, a tall, narrow cupboard holds sports equipment and low shoe racks. The cupboard is painted the same gray as the rest of the woodwork.

left: Easy-to-wash cotton runners are seen all over Scandinavia, and although these are commercially-made, runners are often handed down through the generations. The frugal grandmothers of today's home owners wove their own rugs by hand using recycled fabrics.

right: The beautifully simple wallpaper, printed with a blue trellis pattern on a white background, makes an unassuming foil to the piles of creamy-white china that glint in the sunlight.

traditional patterns

In a northern farmhouse this kitchen's pale blue and gray color scheme is diluted with lots of light-reflecting Scandinavian white, and the soft colors are repeated on the subtle wallpaper that decorates the walls. The simple all-over pattern gives the room a traditional look that sits well with the typical furniture, muslin-curtained windows, and bare wooden floor. Patterned walls have made a comeback in modern interiors recently after being out of fashion for years, but simple geometric designs were common in Swedish country houses, either hand painted or printed by hand with wooden blocks, since the sixteenth century. After the invention of the first commercial wallpaper-printing machine in the early twentieth century, cheaper versions became widely available and it became an established way to decorate any room. The Nordic Museum in Stockholm has a large collection of wallpaper samples that traces its history through the centuries, as well as reconstructed room sets, which make the museum a wonderful place to visit for anyone wanting to trace the authentic development of Swedish style.

modern minimalism

In a contemporary, architect-designed house near London, the play of light through the high, floor-to-ceiling windows changes dramatically throughout the day. Moving from a flat, subdued light in the early morning, by the afternoon shafts of sunlight are streaming into the living room, creating shadows that accentuate the structure of the room. The clean lines of the walls, designed with the severe aesthetic of minimalism in mind, need no other decoration than panels of warm brown color applied in the alcoves to define the spaces, while columns of white throw the light back into the room. The contrast between the internal and external planes is accentuated by the simple change of tone. At night, when the alcoves are lit from above by downlighters, the effect is to bring the eye down to ceiling height.

In a more modest house you can utilize the effect of color against white so that it seems to change the proportions of a room. Paint a chimney breast in a strong tone and you will draw attention to the single architectural feature of an otherwise unremarkable room. Apply warm color like brown, terra cotta, or red to the end walls in a long, narrow room and the room will immediately look less like a corridor. Try painting soft pink on the ceiling of a small, high room with white walls and see how the tall space looks more inviting. Remember that the warmer colors in the spectrum, like reds, pinks, and terra cotta, will come forward, while cool, airy colors, like blues, greens, and lavenders, will recede.

left: A row of over-sized white ceramic lamps throw out pools of light that completely change the effect after dark, making a space that is dramatic by day, intimate and cozy by night.

below: Different surfaces create a variety of textures, adding sensuality and depth to a minimalist room. The reflective surfaces of ceramic, glass, and polished wood contrast with the matte quality of velvet and suede, allowing the eye to be stimulated and relaxed by turn.

color moods

Blending white with carefully selected areas of strong tones is the best way to use bright color without letting it overwhelm a room. The optical effect of a single wall painted in burnt orange, cerulean blue, or chilli-pepper red, when surrounded by white, will focus the eye and make the color more intense. Color can affect your mood too, so it's worth thinking carefully about what shade you intend to use in different spaces. Red and orange are invigorating and rousing and thought to be excellent used in dining rooms because they can stimulate the appetite. Green is the relaxing, balancing color of nature, and is suitable for any room in the house. Blue is the most relaxing of them all, perfect for bedrooms, while yellow has the reputation of encouraging intellectual activity, so think about using it in studies and work areas.

left: A bright orange wall is selected from the many planes of white in this ultra-modern London house. The warmth of the color brings the wall forward, while the whites seem to change hue as daylight moves across the different angles.

right: In Sweden color is used to great effect on the outside of houses, and most exteriors are painted in beautiful hues where the exuberance of the color is often at odds with the calm, pale interiors. This brilliant, blue front door has been faded by the sun of many summers, but still looks radiant.

left: In a cool, dark hallway which gets little light, a vintage red lifebelt warms up the white wall and introduces an element of color as well as being an unusual talking point.

right: The lifebelt, found in a naval antique shop in Stockholm's Gamla Stan, or old town, pays tribute to the fact that the house is situated on a remote island, half an hour by fast boat from the nearest town.

collectible display

Using decorative objects is a great way to bring color into a white space where there's no chance of making use of soft furnishings to provide accent color. Hallways are often long, dark, and uninspiring and can be the perfect place to display interesting collections or a single, quirky piece. Ideas for display can be as wild and wonderful as your imagination; a collection of framed 1940s headscarves, a wooden African mask, or a Japanese silk kimono are just a few ideas, although you will be able to come up with plenty of your own. Others could include hanging a beloved set of vintage hand-painted plates along the hall wall, or exhibiting a pair of colorful but distressed oars from a long-decayed boat. Junk shops and flea markets can yield hidden treasures that will look completely transformed when displayed in an original way.

naturally inspired

right: One of the freshest color combinations must be the merging of green and white, one of nature's most uncomplicated pairings. A branch of white orange blossom in a plain vase is mirrored by the low cup that holds a single rose. The pale green pillow adds a hint of spring to the snow-white bed linen.

below: The simplest lines, taken from traditional Swedish designs, have been used for the painted bedroom furniture in this country farmhouse. The bed, side table, and rocking chair are all new, making this look readily available to anyone.

Bringing the outside in is one of the main preoccupations of the Scandinavians, whose love of nature is legendary. With their experience of long, harsh winters and surrounded by forests and lakes all year round, Nordic people have learned to get along with the cycles of nature. Most city dwellers get away from the stresses of modern life as often as they can, and many have their own house, chalet, or small cabin in the country where they can enjoy the great outdoors, whether it is swimming in a summer lake or skiing in the mountains.

In Sweden, on the outskirts of each city, small plots of land known as "kolonilotts," each with its own "stuga" or tiny cabin, can be seen, where those without the resources to buy a holiday home can grow their own vegetables, set up a table and chairs, and spend summer days away from their apartment. So when it comes to choosing colors for the home, it's not surprising that the colors seen in the natural world should be so much in evidence. The airiness of blue and green, when balanced with pure white, recalls the crispness of mountain scenery in winter or the purity of a spring morning.

In Carl Larsson's paintings, wooden furniture and unfussy wooden paneling painted in these, as well as brighter colors, are seen in many of the rooms along with pale, scrubbed floors and simple woven runners. Many people decorating their homes today in the authentic Swedish style use his paintings as inspiration.

far left: Fresh flowers are a constant reminder of the seasons and you don't have to spend a fortune on large, expensive bouquets to enjoy them. A few summer blossoms from the garden, like these white scabious and purple veronica, look unassuming and delicate next to the bed.

center: A modern wooden bed draws on the traditional designs of Scandinavia for the simplified shapes of the detailing. The paintwork is new, but carefully distressed to appear as if the furniture has been in the family for generations.

left: Beaded paneling—where narrow wooden mouldings are glued to the wall and painted in a contrast color—must be one of the easiest ways to give an authentic Swedish look to any room. Here, green beading against the white wall gives a plain bedroom style and elegance.

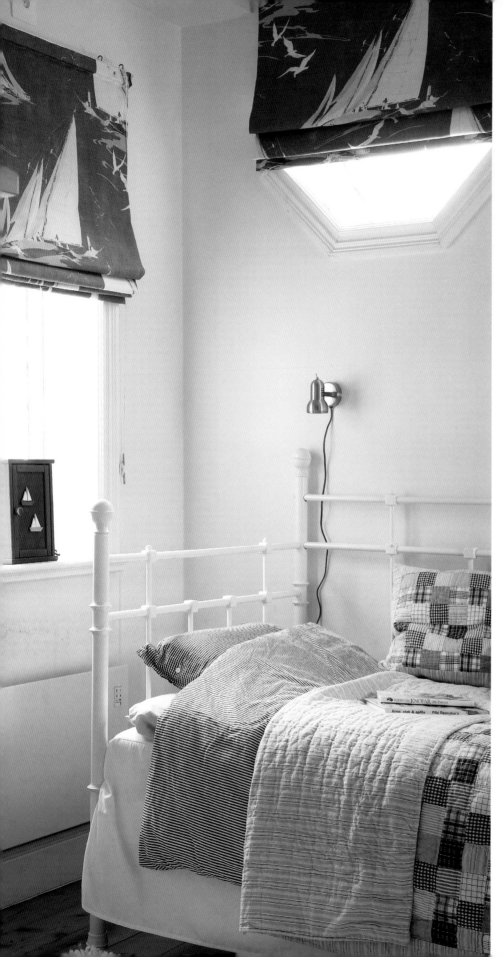

above: On the wall outside a shared bathroom, members of the family have each painted a depiction of the boats that sail or steam their way among the islands of the Stockholm archipelago.

left: A boy's bedroom reflects his love of sailing, and the deep blue of the Roman shades, with their yachting theme, is underlined by the blue-and-white patchwork quilt and denim bed linen. The metal day bed gives a feeling of a ship's railings and the small chrome spotlight has a distinctly nautical air.

above right: A white bathroom has been kept deliberately simple for cleanliness and trouble-free maintenance, but the long, low bench has a set of colorfully striped squab pillows, making it perfect for the youngest members of the family to stand on to be washed and dressed.

children's rooms

When decorating for children and teenagers, it's always fun to come up with a room that will make their own spaces really special and give them their individuality. Conventional rules of good taste can be relaxed; colors can be bolder and fabrics more audacious than in the rest of the house. For younger children, a themed bedroom will appeal to their sense of adventure, and a topic based around a favorite sport, a fantasy world, or a beloved pet can all be starting points. Opt for window fabrics that underpin the theme, selecting a print that sets the tone, and pick wall colors using this fabric as a guide. Co-ordinating fabrics for bed linen and accessories will follow, so choose colors and prints that go with the main material. For a focal point choose a bed that reinforces the look, so in a fairy castle bedroom a white mini four-poster with sheer drapes would be ideal, while for a nautically-themed room, look out for a set of wooden bunk beds complete with ship's ladder.

For older children and teenagers, color can be the focal point, especially if you team brighter hues on the walls with furniture painted in tones that would normally look kitsch or outrageous. But bear in mind that the darkness or lightness of a room depends as much on the quality of natural light as the brightness of the color.

right: Lacking a plain wall in this teenager's bedroom, the bed has been placed in front of the old-style radiator, keeping the sleeper cozy on long winter nights. The unusual color combination of lime-green metal bed, sky blue walls, and white floorboards appears fresh and young without seeming garish.

below: A flat-pack cabinet, painted a strong salmon pink, adds a flash of contrast in the corner of the same bedroom. The vintage mirror, found in a junk shop, is positioned to reflect light into the corner and makes a simple dressing table for make-up.

painted surfaces

Panelled walls are a characteristic feature of many Scandinavian rooms, both traditional and contemporary, which is defined by the fact that most homes are built in wood. Paneling ranges from the elegant Gustavian look with tall rectangular panels of fine molding, to carved panels that normally line the lower part of the walls only. Narrow tongue-and-groove boards are usually mounted vertically and cover the whole wall and often the ceiling, too. Painting the paneling can mean covering the entire surface with a single color, or picking out different tones to make a contrast. But however they are painted, the different planes will catch the light so that a flat wall has a constantly changing surface of light and shadow. This effect can be accentuated by using various paint types, which will give walls anything from a dull matte finish to the soft sheen of silk, or the highly reflective look of gloss. Paint a paneled section in white, but watch how gloss-painted panels will stand out from a matte wall above. Apply a duck-egg blue eggshell paint to tongue and groove and see how its soft luster reflects the light and emphasizes the vertical grooves.

left: The walls of this staircase have been lined with a narrow tongue-and-groove paneling. It's an authentic finish for an old farmhouse in Sweden and one that was originally only used on ceilings.

right: In a contemporary conversion of a 1920s house in London, sliding wall panels conceal and reveal a tiny bathroom and storage cupboard behind. When closed, the panels become a solid wall whose painted finish reflect maximum light into the tiny bedroom with its blue bed linen.

bold prints

Cotton fabrics have been used in Scandinavian homes since block-printed and painted patterns were imported from India and China at the beginning of the eighteenth century, although these were always an expensive luxury. These fabrics were later copied within Europe and Sweden. When cotton became cheaper to import from the American colonies and printing technology improved, low-cost printed cottons were produced at home and became immensely popular throughout all strata of society. These days the wheel has turned full circle, and many of the early designs are being printed once more in India, sometimes screen printed, but often printed by hand using carved wooden blocks.

above left: In a guest bedroom, the entire wall behind the bed has been covered with padded fabric. This makes a comfortable and insulated wall, which is warm and cozy to lean against. Two downlighters positioned above throw shafts of light on the bed for reading.

above: The striking floral fabric depicts green and white flowers which have a hand-painted look, but have been screen-printed onto the natural linen ground. The contemporary lamp highlights the sage greens of the leaf pattern.

Printed wallpapers also became popular as technology improved in the nineteenth century, although the earliest form of wall covering was, in fact, printed or painted fabric simply pinned in place with copper pins. Covering a wall with fabric is still a warm and beautiful way to decorate a room, and although it is usually done by a professional, it is not impossible to attempt yourself. Join fabric widths together first and staple the fabric to narrow wooden battens screwed to the wall. The fabric must be stretched to look completely taut and is not a job to be undertaken without practice, but it is a unique and individual way to enhance a feature wall.

above left: Traditional wallpaper designs are still available, and the owners of this house, built in 1890, have used a pattern that would have been very much the style when the house was first lived in.

above: Block-printed in India onto hand woven linen, this one-color fabric makes the perfect pair of airy, unlined curtains when clipped to a rail with brass clips. The striped pillow is hand printed onto the same fabric, and has the modest quality of old Swedish sack cloth.

left: Built from materials quarried nearby in Dorset, England, the wall of this garden room, which was originally on the outside of the cottage, is softened by strands of jasmine that form a graceful tracery across the rough-hewn stone.

right: Shafts of sunshine filter gently through the windows onto the stone floor, contributing a play of light and shadow to the mottled surface. The slabs have been laid in an irregular pattern, which help to give the floor a rustic, aged appearance.

light on texture

When color is at a minimum, the quality of light contributes greatly to the surfaces it falls on. The swirls of embroidered voile, the texture of hand-woven linen, or the shapes of a fretwork panel—all depend on light for their defining characteristic.

tone on tone

After she had completely renovated its angular rooms, the stylist owner of this London attic apartment was left with a living space that is refreshingly spare and filled with soft light. Low walls and sloping ceilings were painted brilliant white, and their unadorned surfaces give full play to the planes of shadow as the light changes. Furnishing the living room with contemporary furniture has underlined its calculated simplicity, but it has none of the uncomfortable starkness that can be associated with

above: A low-level gray sofa is piled comfortably with soft pillows of varying sizes. The pillows are carefully chosen from a restrained palette, but it is tone, rather than color, that defines the room. Ultra-contemporary pieces like the Plexiglas side tables and Charles Eames chair sit back modestly, allowing the couch to take center stage.

minimalism. On the contrary, the use of layered neutrals and natural fabrics gives it a sensual quality that invites you to relax and unwind, and the foliage of the potted olive tree introduces a charming touch of nature to the gardenless apartment. The fundamental principles of the room have all the elements of the Scandinavian look—white painted walls, modest window treatments, and a basically uncluttered feel—but the look is cool, contemporary, and timeless.

above left: Linen pillows made from old monogramed sheets and a hand-woven woollen throw give a vintage feel to the modern sofa. The combination of textures, from smooth to coarse, is accentuated by directional light from the window.

above: With no walls to hang paintings, a clever solution was to stack old, gilded picture frames in one corner. The shapes break up the bare expanse of wall and their battered edges and distressed embellishment add a variety of texture.

woven furniture

The earthy texture of hand-woven rattan exudes a warmth that is redolent of the tropical environments where this natural fiber was grown, and its long, flexible strands allow it to be shaped into chairs, sofas, tables, and storage boxes, making this one of the most versatile of materials. The art of weaving is one of man's earliest achievements, and detailed baskets were woven from raw vegetable fibers well before the development of pottery.

In the Philippines and Indonesia, local people have long used the plentiful supplies of bamboo and rattan to weave intricate furniture, both for their own use and to use for trading with other villages and settlements. It was only when intrepid travelers began to explore the world in the sixteenth century that wicker furniture was seen by Europeans, although for centuries many travelers were much more interested in buying spices and other valuable goods than woven furniture, as few people realized its appeal. By the nineteenth century, however, wicker furniture had become very popular in Europe and the USA, and furniture made from it was (and still is) most commonly used either in the garden or on a shady veranda or conservatory as it is so light, durable, and easily moveable.

The range of natural materials used for weaving is much more diverse today than in the past, with the introduction of sea grass, water hyacinth, and banana fiber, as well as the man-made wire-and-paper material invented by Marshall Burns Lloyd in 1917, now known as Lloyd Loom. Contemporary and sleek, many of today's woven furniture designs are well-suited for a modern interior with their innovative shapes and unique surface textures.

right: Fine strands of twisted sea grass are wound into narrow ropes and woven into a chunky, basket-work design on this contemporary armchair. The play of light and shadow highlights the wonderfully tactile surface.

below: A brick wall has been painted white in this Victorian apartment just outside London. The texture of the woven armchair contrasts beautifully with the texture of the brickwork and the grain of the floorboards, but the natural palette keeps it all subtly understated.

decorative framing

Alleviating the starkness of a white wall can mean more than just hanging a single painting or print, and a diverse set of framed pictures will reflect light and add texture. There are no precise formulae to hanging pictures, but there are a few tips. Pick a favorite piece to go in the center of the display and radiate frames outward. It also helps to alternate dark and light, large and small to make the collection look alive. A compilation of similar subjects can be hung much closer together than a varied selection, so a good trick is to find art that has a common theme—and always hang pictures at eye level.

left: A set of framed pictures gravitate around a focal point —an antique mirrored light fitting. The works encompass photographs, pastel sketches, and line drawings, but each one is a human portrait.

left: This contemporary Scandinavian hanging bookshelf holds books in a stack against a plain wall. The books are well-organized and easy to find, but have a very different, textural quality provided by the unusual vertical shelving system.

right: A pair of Fortuny-inspired pendant lamps, with embroidered silk shades, are placed on the sill of a tiny window where the shades hang down against the wall below. Displayed completely out of context, the intricate webbing, long tassels, and Venetian embroidery can be appreciated for their own sake.

far right: In this artist's house, *Robinia* stems and pine needle bundles are bound with wire and stand along the window ledge of the studio. They make an unusual and beautiful still life silhouetted against the light.

contained display

It's always a joy to collect things that catch your eye—a handful of beautifully colored dried leaves on a country walk, a vintage lamp discovered in a favorite flea market, or simply to indulge your passion for art books. These things add immeasurably to the quality of life, and we all need to gather things around us that speak of our individual enthusiasms. But finding places to display our collections can prove more difficult, especially if you live in a modern house or apartment rather than in an old building with plenty of architectural features. You may find yourself short of a mantelpiece, or even a decent alcove where you can build a set of bookshelves. Look for unusual ways to show off your treasures; thinking outside the box can make the simplest object look like an art piece.

textured panels

Swedish Gustavian painted furniture, with its hand-carved decoration and cool, pale colors, was directly influenced by the more costly furniture of the neo-classical period in France and Italy. King Gustav III was only twenty-five when he returned from a study trip to France in 1771, bringing with him examples of the style which had so impressed him. Although hugely influential throughout the country, the average owners of manor houses couldn't afford the gilded furniture they admired, so country craftsmen cleverly imitated the look. Using native pine instead of

mahogany, they built beautifully-carved furniture and painted it pale blue, gray, and weathered white, and the Gustavian Provincial Style was born.

It's a style that still has enormous popularity today, and influences interior designers throughout the world. The owner of this country kitchen is a furniture designer herself, and her collections owe much of their detail to the furniture of the past. Using the diamond center panel which is seen on so many provincial dressers and cabinets, she has created a modern kitchen with all the advantages of today's technology, but one whose design pays tribute to the craftsmen of the past.

left: It's possible to design a kitchen like this for yourself with medium denisty fiberboard replacement paneled doors. Ask a skilled carpenter to make thin, ribbed panels that can be fixed in place and paint all the doors and units in Gustavian gray. Then simply add a set of antique-looking handles.

right: The textural detail of the molded diamonds in the center of the fielded panels is thrown into stark relief as light enters through the window. It's a traditional motif which is seen on highly-sought-after antique furniture.

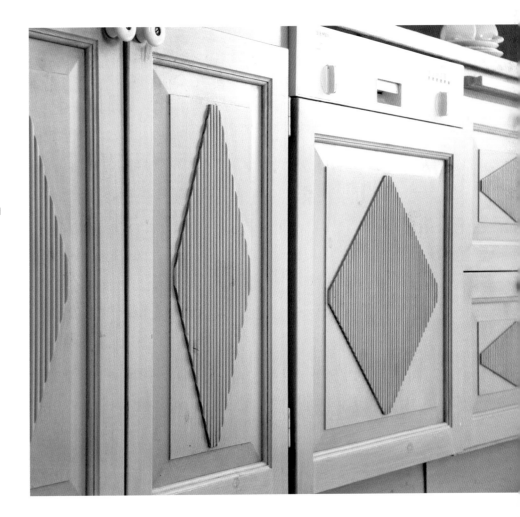

faux texture

Traditionally, Swedish country farmhouses, and homes belonging to the well-off merchant classes, were painted with a wide variety of paint effects, mostly executed by itinerant decorators who specialized in the different techniques. The costly materials of marble, mahogany and even birch, so beloved of the wealthy landowners, were out of reach of most country people in the late eighteenth and nineteenth centuries, but much desired nevertheless. Most had never even seen the real thing (and neither had the decorators!), but this didn't deter them from making a good attempt at creating faux effects. "Marble" walls were particularly popular, and the enthusiastically vivid colors, painted directly onto wooden, planked walls, are utterly charming in their directness.

Skansen, created by Arthur Hazelius in 1891, is Stockholm's open-air museum of houses. It is here that houses from all over Sweden have been reconstructed and restored, and there are many fine examples of faux-painted walls and furniture to be seen there. One of these is the Ekshärad farmhouse, built in the 1820s. The house as it is seen at Skansen today reflects the interior of the 1850s, when it was lived in by the district judge. Pine beds are painted to resemble birch, a desk is painted to look like mahogany, and a writing table makes a wonderful imitation of alder wood. The halls are marbled with a hardly a nod to the real thing, and the splatter-painted kitchen is a typical Scandinavian paint effect, produced when paints of different shades are flicked directly onto a plain wall using birch twigs.

above: A battered sunhat that has seen service for many summers hangs on a square-pegged wooden rail.

left: The planked walls of this farmhouse entrance hall have been decorated with different tones of gray and white, flicked directly onto the painted wood. The painting is new, but it faithfully copies the traditional splatter paint effect. The sturdy, rough-hewn planks are part of the original construction of the house.

right: Gray-marbled door panels and the edge of the staircase have been painted by a contemporary painter with a much more sophisticated hand than the early decorators. The beading, picked out in dark red and gray paintwork, lends an authentic feel to the hallway that is respectful to the house's roots.

above: An old table found at auction, with a pretty, scalloped edge around the top, was painted white to fit into the rest of the room. It's a good approach to adopt, and will give any odd, junk-shop piece a new lease of life.

right: A local carpenter made the double-fold shutters to fit the pair of windows in the bedrooms as well as the radiator covers. Find flat-pack radiator covers in your local DIY store, or order them to your own measurements over the internet to get the same look.

white on white

White-painted elements in a restful guest bedroom illustrate the classic Swedish decorating trait of arranging furniture and objects with perfect symmetry. In the Gustavian interior, furniture was pushed against the wall, and everything arranged with a precise, symmetrical touch. In modest country farmhouses and royal palaces alike, you will find regularity and balance in the way things are arranged. Painted wooden chairs stand perfectly square either side of a bureau, two mirrors stand sentinel on both sides of a doorway, and two tiny round tables echo one another across a draped bed. Even smaller decorative objects are arranged to mirror one another—candlesticks always in pairs on a table for instance. It's a simple technique to emulate, but one which immediately gives an impression of order and calm.

The hinged slats of these American-style shutters have a dual purpose at the windows. They provide privacy at night and fold completely back from the window in the daytime, allowing light to flood in unrestrictedly. In the early mornings the horizontal painted slats catch the light as it creeps through, making a pattern of pale bands on the wall. The panels of trellis-work over the radiators, which bring a classical allusion, make a feature of the otherwise unprepossessing radiators and add a defining contrast as they form diamonds of shadow between the paler cross bars. Perfectly symmetrical, the window joinery frames a white-painted table with scalloped top that becomes the focal point of the room when it is topped with a vase of brilliantly-colored garden flowers.

Ready-made off-the-shelf doors make ideal fronts for a built-in closet in a bedroom or dressing room. Slatted louver doors are usually available untreated or already primed, and come in a wide variety of sizes. Used from floor to ceiling, as here, there are no dusty tops to keep clean, and the closets behind accommodate plenty of hanging space, with shelves above for items that are not used every day.

above: The slats of the doors reflect light in regular strips that break up the expanse of wall, enhanced by the simplicity of small round door knobs.

left: A deep-pile wool rug adds texture to the stripped wooden floorboards and gives a sensual feel under bare feet.

above: Making the most of the extra hanging space, the owner of this dressing room enjoys showing off her collection of beautifully understated clothes. The dresses are designer statements that are far too lovely to hide away in the wardrobe and bring an ethereal quality with their soft, crumpled textures.

silken textures

Using fabrics with an integral sheen, like silks and satins or their man-made equivalents, brings another dimension to the meaning of texture. Matte, hand-woven fabrics have a crunchy, satisfying appeal of their own, but the reflective effects of silken cloth add immeasurably to the quality of light in a room. Even when used as a flat sheet, a satin fabric will bend and shimmer as it folds around the contours below. But with an embroidered or stitched surface texture, it will break up light, making myriad shadows.

The simplest of quilting, like large squares that attach a top layer of satin to the padded interlining underneath, forms more than just the geometric shapes of the stitch lines. Each pucker and crease are exaggerated as light runs across the surface like water, running into rivulets and forming tiny pools. Sewn into tiny pleats on a pillow, light is regimented and disciplined along orderly channels as it follows the highlighted rim of each. Embroidery adds another dimension to the polish of a silk fabric; the raised thread punctuates the smoothness of the surface, adding stitch by stitch, a rhythm and cadence that tells its own story.

right: The gleam of the shiny bed linen is accentuated by the matte surface of the walls in this feminine and sophisticated bedroom. The old garden chair, with its distressed and battered appearance, only serves to underline the refined nature of the pillows and quilt.

far right: The soft lavender hue of a pleated pillow forms a pleasing contrast to the gleaming whiteness of an embroidered fabric, and pale tones of each are reflected in the folds of the other.

above left: Tiny fragments of crab claws and shells, so broken they are barely recognizable and well onto their way to becoming sand, were picked up on a remote beach on a Scottish island. Mounted onto watercolor paper in orderly rows, each sliver assumes the preciousness of a rare fossil.

above: Embroidered ribbons are curled together on a reflective dish and echoes of their delicate tracery can be seen as ghostly shadows.

left: Handmade soaps with embossed patterns resemble fragrant Turkish delight, and with their powdery surfaces look almost good enough to eat.

right: The epitome of the domestic life; a toothbrush in a glass, colored shampoo bottles, and a soap dispenser arranged on shelves take on the quality of translucent gems with the sun shining through them.

accidental arrangements

We bring order to our lives, tidying and putting away, without necessarily having any intention to make pleasing displays. The bathroom needs cleaning, so we fold the towels in a pile and arrange shampoo bottles on the shelf. An assortment of ribbons lies on the workroom table, so they are rolled and placed on a tray where they can easily be found later when we need them. But sometimes, something magical happens. The assemblage of textures and surfaces, matte and shiny, hard and soft, fall into interesting conjunctions that we notice with a passing quiet pleasure. A small detail of our domestic life is suddenly imbued with beauty. This is a subtle message that the everyday can be made to be extraordinary if we can just take a moment to appreciate it. We may not think of ourselves as artists, and we might not think of sitting down to make a painting. But life can be gently tweaked to bring out our innate creativity wherever we find ourselves.

Once this awareness has been cultivated, we can start to subtly change the way we see things. A bag of vegetables from the market might be thrust into a box in the pantry, but what if the best of them were to be displayed on the kitchen table instead? Shiny, purple eggplants next to the gloss of red and green tomatoes on the vine. The white florets of a cauliflower against the knobbliness of a yellow gourd. As we move through our day, such small things can give us a delight that will make the most of every moment.

delicately embossed

Sunshine filtering through the flimsy folds of a muslin blind on a summer's day, or highlighting the gently billowing drapery of a pair of sheer curtains will always change the quality of light in a room. When the fabric is embroidered, the fact that it is held up against the light outlines every swirl and leaf, and pure white embroidery on white fabric is an unbeatable combination. The fine tracery of pattern is put under the spotlight and seen at its best advantage and it is only the light behind it that can bring out the full beauty of the design. Clipped up onto a narrow pole, a piece of embellished voile is all that's needed at many windows. The insubstantiality of the shade may not give privacy, but in Scandinavia this is rarely an issue and most folk are perfectly comfortable sitting in a living room looking on to the street without heavy drapes to protect them from passers-by. For those of use wishing to hide just a little, a thin white roller shade can be fixed behind and we can have the best of both worlds.

The concept of white-on-white patterning can be found in unexpected places in an old house if you pause to look for examples of architectural detailing. Georgian and Victorian architects were always keen to decorate the edges of rooms with plaster cornices, and although they were often seen painted in contrast colors, there's nothing to beat a coat of white paint to highlight the decorative detailing.

above: For a crisp, sharp effect, stripping off the old paint from a Victorian plaster cornice is the only option, and there is no short cut to doing this. But years of paint have softened and blurred the contours of these moldings, which has given them an antique charm of their own.

right: A panel of modern cotton voile has an embroidered border that is prettily displayed as it folds over a wooden pole. The panel is rolled by hand and caught up underneath by a set of narrow white ribbons.

far right: This antique fabric, brought from the owner's family estate, was too valuable to be cut and sewn, so it was made into a mere slip of a window dressing by hand-stitching it in place over a narrow metal rod.

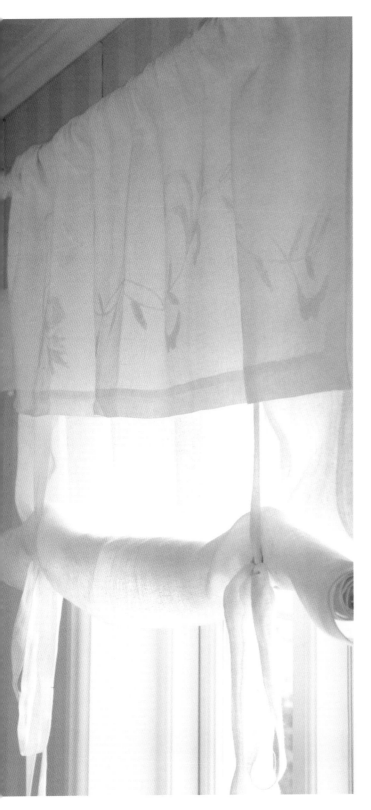

left: The upturned bowl of a glossy chrome lamp reflects, in miniature, a replica of the glass-roofed studio in which it hangs.

right: The column of a mirrored glass candlestick with its fluid, sculptural quality stands as a decorative object in its own right.

reflected light

Shining surfaces pick up each stray gleam of light and illuminate their surroundings. A lusterous candlestick, a sparkling chandelier or a polished mirror—all will expand the perceived sense of space and add luminosity to a room.

above: A striking antique picture frame, with the original painting removed, has been fitted with mirror glass. Hung above a contemporary fireplace, the juxtaposition of old and new makes an interesting combination.

left: Built in the 1920s, this studio in London is part of a complex of houses and studios conceived as an artist's community. Today the studio is used as a bright, airy living area, into which light pours through the glass roof on its north-facing side. The mirror above the fireplace throws light back into the white room.

mirror, mirror

There's no better way of introducing extra ambient light than with the use of strategically-placed mirrors. Mirrors maximize the potential of every bit of illumination, whether it's the brightness of sunlight pouring through a window, or the radiance of candlelight. Placed on the wall opposite a window or fixed above a mantelpiece, a mirror increases the amount of light and brings a dark space to life, both in the daytime and at night.

A large expanse of mirrored glass can also double the apparent size of a small room, especially when fixed to a bedroom or bathroom wall in a contemporary setting; and a collection of interesting vintage mirrors makes a resplendent display if hung close together on a large surface area.

Mirrors have been used since the time of ancient Egypt, when they were made from molten bronze or copper, but after the invention of glass, the Romans found that coating one side with metal made a useful reflective surface. Beautiful Venetian mercury glass, produced since the sixteenth century, was manufactured by coating the back of hand-blown glass with a mixture of tin and mercury. These days, mirrors are made with a thin layer of molten aluminum or silver sprayed onto the back of flat plate glass to form a crystal-clear image.

reflective highlights

Once you begin to notice which materials reflect light, it's a small step to start using them to bring a lusterous look to all areas of the house. Whether your home is a contemporary living space or a more traditional interior, there are many modern surfaces that can be brought together

above: Used as a splashback, sink and worktop in this London kitchen, sheets of stainless steel glimmer with a soft light that is bounced back from the chrome faucets, aluminum colander, and black, shiny bowl in the window.

to provide polished highlights. The burnished face of a stainless steel worktop or the polished curve of a set of chrome faucets will make a tiny kitchen area shimmer, while a dark hallway can be brought to life with the addition of a gilt-framed mirror beside the door.

above: A garden door stands wide open, allowing summer light to illuminate this hallway. The large mirror on the wall serves two purposes, making the space look larger as well as doubling the amount of light.

Using reflective surfaces in unusual places can make usually overlooked areas of your home into something much more special. Fixing mirror glass in unexpected places, for instance, brings in a startling element that can kick-start a room from the ordinary to the surprisingly unique. Reflective mirrors positioned behind bookshelves or under a window will bounce light back so that the usual boundaries of a room are softened and lose definition. It appears that the space is twice the actual size, and one room seems to be two. Experiment by fixing a sheet of mirror inside an alcove, on the underside of shelves, or inside an unused fireplace and try out the effects for yourself.

right: American diner chairs, made from softly reflective aluminum, make a gleaming alternative to more traditional designs in this kitchen with its pine wooden table.

below left: Positioned behind the sink in an ultra-modern kitchen, mirror glass gives the illusion that the room continues to another space beyond the wall.

below: Stainless steel, glass, and white china combine to throw off myriad highlights. Stainless steel is fixed to the underside of the shelf, giving even more emphasis to the shimmer.

vintage sparkle

Scandinavians live close to nature and try to bring the qualities of light that they see around them indoors wherever possible: sunlight sparkling and glittering over the surface of a lake, dewdrops glistening on a spider's web, and the shimmer of an icicle in the moonlight. Many homes in Sweden have an antique chandelier, with crystals that sparkle as they slowly move in the air, but even a single crystal hung at a window will refract any stray beam that comes its way, often throwing a glorious rainbow across the room into the bargain.

Antique cut glass, like carved ice or diamonds, has a multitude of different planes that flash as light passes over it, but a pressed glass decanter from a thrift store will shine and gleam to almost the same degree if it's kept clean and polished. Collections of old glass look wonderful if they are displayed together, so seek out a single type and group them on a window ledge, side table, or shelf.

left: The aged patina of an eighteenth-century mirror reflects the room with a misty gaze. The gilded frame has all the hallmarks of the neo-classical era, with its cameo of King Gustav III, laurel leaves, and crimped ribbon trims, while the gold leaf softly glows in the afternoon sunlight.

above right: A set of tiny vases are each just big enough to hold one sprig of eucalyptus; it's an understated way to display flowers or foliage.

above far right: A traditional candle-shade light fitting has extra wire arms that hold a set of shining crystals. In the daytime, the crystals glint in the sun, while at night it is the light from the lamps that set off their radiance.

below right: This collection of vintage glass bud vases from the 1950s and 60s have been sourced from thrift stores and flea markets over the years. The heavy bases are found in every color, with more added to the set as they are found.

below far right: They might have been bought inexpensively, but when grouped together, five pressed-glass decanters make a stunning display on a side table with their diversity of shapes and moldings.

Glitzy clothes are too good to be hidden away in a closet, especially as they are unlikely to be worn very often. So pick out a showy pair of shoes and keep them where they can twinkle—they are great fun to look at and have around, even if you know you'll rarely wear them. A satin slip or a chiffon gown—why not indulge your fantasies and enjoy the sheer luxury of vintage clothes as decorative objects. Flea markets and second-hand clothes shops are a rich hunting ground for these flights of fancy, and if you can ignore the dress size and concentrate on the beauty of the textiles, even better.

In the 1930s, clothes gained most of their allure from the sheen of the fabrics, and furniture from the same era used reflective surfaces to bring glamour into the interior. Mirrored tables and desks made enchanting additions to an Art Deco room, and although vintage originals can be very expensive, with the recent revival of interest in the look, new pieces are easy to get hold of today.

far left: Keep vintage dresses on display, but use them sparingly. Two or three pale garments, a couple of strings of pearls, and a line up of glamorous shoes is all it takes.

center left: A round glass knob makes even the most mundane piece of door furniture a thing of beauty and light.

left: These may not be shoes that go dancing every night, but they are sensational with their marquesite-studded straps.

right: A French chest of drawers has been painted and distressed with silvery-gray paint, which gives it a gently reflective surface. The mirror above is a decorative, vintage piece from the 1940s.

bathroom surfaces

Tiles are essential when it comes to choosing a waterproof splashback around basins, bath tubs, and showers, but the selection of materials, color, and surface texture needs to be in line with the overall look of the scheme. A simple white country bathroom only asks for a set of plain ceramic tiles to be fitted to the wall around wet areas. Laid in a regular

above: An antique light fitting above a gold mirror adds form and texture to this white bathroom.

above left: The sheen of the white tiles softly reflect light, and the matching pair of mirrors form pools of illumination.

pattern, the look is traditional and unassuming, especially when teamed with painted wooden cabinets to soften it. An architect-designed, urban bathroom demands something more dramatic however, and sealed limestone with its natural texture and glossy surface, creates a streamlined, contemporary effect.

above left: The basin and surfaces are carved from a single piece of limestone, whose polished surface gleams with light.

above: This fabulous sunken bath, in a house near London, has been designed with a combination of limestone tiles and dark-toned mosaics. In the ceiling, a circular glass panel lets in a striking shaft of sunlight.

left: Even without a fire, an empty fireplace can look welcoming if it's filled with logs. The radiance of a few candles on the mantelpiece fills the room with a gentle luminosity.

right: A pair of vintage sundae dishes lit from within by tea lights show off the texture of the glass and make an attractive and interesting display.

night light and firelight

Before the advent of electric light, people relied on candles and firelight to illuminate their homes after dark. These days we have a choice, but the soft glow of a real flame in the evenings will always be a welcome supplement.

candlelight

Use your imagination and you'll be able to come up with a host of different ways to put candles at center stage. On the dining table, a formal tablecenter has always involved flowers and tall dinner candles, but a low set of decorative votive holders, molded glass jars with a small candle in each, or a hand-painted plate set with a circle of tea lights will guarantee a flickering glow that will give even a simple weekday family supper a special-occasion feel.

Every room in the house can benefit from a little candlelight. Baths are more soothing and sensuous with one or two scented candles burning on a shelf; in the bedroom a gentle candle flame will give off a romantic, peaceful aura, and in the living room a few pillar candles set on a mantelpiece or low coffee table will immeasurably add to the atmosphere on a cold winter's evening.

Finding containers to keep candles safely away from flammable surfaces has a double benefit. A hot tea light can damage a polished table top, and it looks so much more decorative if it's placed inside a small holder. This can be anything from an antique china cup to a large, flat sea shell. One of the most important things to remember is that no candle should ever be left unattended. If you leave the room, it's imperative that all candles are blown out before you go.

left: An array of tea lights in decorative glass jars are set on the table in a Swedish dining room. When the table is laid for dinner, each place setting will have its own small light source.

right: Wonderfully simple, but effective nonetheless. A scented candle is set in the middle of a collection of shells. The battered enamel bowl that contains them was found in a junk shop and the whole display makes an individual centerpiece.

below: The Swedish-style of this London living room relies on white curtains and covers, and a bare painted floor. The pitcher of foliage and flowers from the garden and pools of candlelight make a tranquil ambience for a summer's evening.

festive lights

There are always those special mealtimes that seem to cry out for a touch of extravagance, and throughout Scandinavia Christmas and New Year's Eve are marked by family and friends getting together to eat and celebrate. The colors of the winter landscape, with its snow-covered forests and frozen lakes, can inform interior decorations at this time of year, and for a stylish departure from the more traditional red and green theme at Christmas, a white table decorated with silver makes an enchantingly understated setting. Candles are obligatory, and tall dinner candles in polished candlesticks give a shimmering height to the center of the table, while a set of tea lights scattered about the white cloth introduces lights at a lower level.

Large displays of flowers are often considered de rigeur for a Christmas tablecenter, perhaps with a few candles pushed in between, but they can look overpowering and make it difficult to chat to fellow guests across the table. Make a simple and effective decoration by soaking a ring of florist's foam in water before placing it on a large plate. Short stems of greenery, such as variegated ivy, eucalyptus and rosemary, can be pushed in all around the ring until it is completely covered. Place a large white church candle in the center and tuck in a selection of small silver baubles to nestle in the foliage.

above: Light seeps through the sides of delicate shell napkin rings, used here to enclose night lights, and mirrored mats placed underneath make small, silvered squares on this New Year's table. The dark, glossy plates are highlighted by the glimmering dinner candles.

left: A French linen sheet makes the perfect start to dressing this long trestle table for New Year's Eve. In the centet, a handful of eucalyptus leaves make an understated touch of foliage with a distinctly Swedish flavor.

right: Giving the table an extra festive touch, a glass bowl of silvery baubles reflects the candlelight. It's a decoration that takes only moments to assemble, but one which immediately says it's a celebration.

winter whites

In a contemporary living room, celebratory elements introduced to decorate the room at Christmas need to be bold, with shapes strong enough to hold their own in a defiantly minimal space. Clean, uncluttered lines and raw surfaces such as slate and wood insist on chunky decorations, and large candles, log fires, and graphic shapes stand on their own merits in an uncompromising way. In this architect-designed family home near London, the materials and colors speak of

above: The textures of the white leather chair and deep pile rug add their own resonance to the winter references in the room, suggesting rolling hills blanketed with snow and the frosted tips of grasses.

natural forms and authentic materials. White is the background, with warm neutral tones provided by wood, slate, and a rich brown wall color. The contemporary fireplace has realistic ceramic logs with gas flames that flare and leap convincingly, giving out a flickering warm light on a cold winter's day. The stacked birch logs to the side of the fireplace are only for show, but their silvery bark tells of Nordic forests and clean, cold air.

above left: On the single block of wood that acts as a mantelpiece, a collection of Ethiopian Coptic crosses made of silver form a delicate tracery against the white wall, with a structure that is reminiscent of snowflakes and ice crystals.

above: This hand-carved ibex head, brought back from a trip to Africa, looks spectacular against the dark wall. With its dramatic white horns, it has a certain affinity with the snowy wastes and herds of the north.

gustavian retreat

Many houses in Sweden have a wooden guest house in the garden (sometimes even two or three), where visitors and returning children can stay or take up residence for the summer. This charming two-roomed house is built right on the water in the small island harbour of Vaxholm, near Stockholm. Up until a few years ago the house was lived in by an elderly woman and the wallpaper, furniture, and lights, all in the eighteenth-century Gustavian style, remain intact. Today it is the annexe to a nearby family home, and is used on summer evenings for entertaining friends. With no electricity, the house is lit purely by candlelight, giving it an authentic atmosphere. Candlelight was the only form of lighting in the past, and the small flames could provide twice as much light if set against the reflective surfaces of crystal, silver, or brass.

left: Everything is geared to making the interior of this tiny room as light as possible. Brass sconces on the walls hold a double candle, and the gilded mirror provides a pool of light.

above right: A shimmering chandelier is laden with crystals which pick up each tiny gleam of light from the lit candles and set them glistening.

right: The two-roomed house is set right on the water, and its dark lower floor, lit with candles, makes a welcoming place for an evening supper with friends.

electric light

In nature light changes constantly, giving us variety and subtlety throughout the day. If we are to feel energized and happy, artificial lighting needs to be chosen to provide as much depth of contrast as can be found outdoors, rather than simply instaling light bulbs as a way to see what we are doing after dark. When the days are short, good indoor lighting can provide a richness of visual experience that makes the interior relaxing and welcoming, as well as allowing us to work and read comfortably. It was only a hundred years ago that the electric light was invented and it revolutionized the way interiors were decorated. Before then, the grime produced by oil or gas lighting necessitated decorating with dark colors, but with the advent of the new, clean light bulb, it became possible to use white and light shades for the first time.

Modern lighting has come a long way since the first low-voltage bulbs were strung around a room. Bulbs today are brighter, so need to be concealed in some way to avoid unwelcome glare. The reason for the popularity of the ubiquitous Japanese white paper shade is the way they transform a dazzling central light bulb into a globe of soft white light. Recessed low-voltage downlights give the equivalent of bright daylight that makes it easy to work in the kitchen, and the latest wall lights wash walls with diffused light that gives a good background light as well as a restful ambience.

above: It's a tradition in Scandinavia for lamps to be placed just inside a window so that the house will greet visitors arriving in the dark and cold. This antique light gives a soft radiance that sends out a message of welcome.

left: A decorative wall light shades the light source and prevents glare, but the brass spokes allow points of light to radiate outward, creating a sun ray effect on the wall.

far left: Positioned under a staircase just inside the entrance to the living room, the wall light illuminates a dark corner and adds a visually interesting feature to an area that could easily have been dull and uninteresting.

TO STUDIOS
B,C,E,F,G,X.
ONLY

left: Dappled light on an old wall in a shady spot makes a relaxing place to sit with the morning paper and a cup of coffee.

right: The flower heads of ox-eye daisies, picked when they are fully open during the morning, float in a terra cotta dish. It's a simple water feature that can uplift even the tiniest balcony.

light outside

From breakfast on the terrace to drinks by the water, the Scandinavian way of life means spending as much time as possible out of doors, ensuring that no moment of precious summer light is wasted.

the veranda

When natural light is scarce for most of the year, making the most of your outside spaces in summer becomes a necessity. The owners of this Swedish country house, originally built in 1890 as a summer home, used early photographs for reference when designing and building a wooden veranda in the original style. This is now used as a garden room and outdoor living area.

above left: The horizontal wooden matchboarding is typical of Swedish houses built at this period and its texture makes an interesting backdrop for an ornamental birch-bark heart that echoes the folk art of the country. A display of pelargoniums and hydrangeas adds a splash of color.

above: Even on a summer's day there can be a chill to contend with when you sit outdoors, especially when the north wind blows in over the sea. With warm blankets at hand and unobtrusive wall heaters, there's nothing to stop you sitting out until late to enjoy the light nights that are such compensation for long, dark winters.

right: On the wall of the house is hung an old-fashioned, gray-painted peg rail with a shelf that doubles as a display area and utilitarian hat stand.

left: A large glasshouse in a Swedish seaside town stands at the bottom of the garden against the boundary wall. It's a peaceful place to retire to in the late evening, when the last rays of the northern sun hit the wall and the sea breezes are cool.

below: Furniture imported from the Far East gives the greenhouse a colonial air. A wooden bench sofa is strewn with pillows and covered with a white cotton throw, and the garden chair, faded to a silvery gray by the sun, is padded with a pair of mattress pillows.

sheltered corners

Although hot weather is becoming more frequent due to climate change, northern gardens can sometimes be chilly in summer, especially after dusk, and finding a spot out of the wind where you can sit and enjoy the garden might mean being creative with the spaces you have. Originally the greenhouse and orangery were designed to house tender tropical plants in winter, although the cost of maintaining and heating them meant they were only for the wealthy. Orange and lemon trees, palms, and even orchids would be grown, and the larger plants put outside for the summer. In winter, when large pots were brought inside, south-facing windows would let in the sun and the glasshouse would be heated by a spirit stove.

In a very hot summer, a modern south-facing conservatory can overheat, and in winter can be too cold to use, but with a few practical adjustments all can be made to be comfortable and relaxing places to sit in. A set of bespoke shades can be well worth the expense in summer, especially inside a glass roof, as the light will be diffused and keep out the greater part of the heat. Stone or terra cotta tiles on the floor will soak up spring and autumn sun, helping to warm the space, while an electric convector heater will maintain a comfortable temperature. Finding the right furniture is crucial, and a comfortable seating area with washable covers will enhance the enjoyment. Add a low table and a few lanterns for evening, and a garden retreat is ready for use all year round.

below: Out of the wind, a purpose-built corner seat has been tucked under a pergola. The oversized linen pillows are stored inside until a good day, when they are carried outside to make a wonderfully comfortable area for relaxing.

light on water

The Baltic sea, bordered in Scandinavia by Sweden and Finland, looks more like a lake than a sea. Its low salt content allows reeds and grasses to thrive down to the water's edge so the shoreline of the islands near Stockholm is mainly green and surrounded by forest. With so many vacation homes overlooking the water, it's a common sight to see wooden jetties stretching out into the sea as moorings for the sailing and motor boats that provide transport and recreation. Any waterside home in Scandinavia has its decked sitting areas, furnished with white-painted furniture at the ready for watching the sun go down.

above: Light sparkles on the water around a long wooden pontoon, with its open pavilion. The seats inside are perfectly placed for watching the boats go by in the water beyond the island.

above: Bright blue and red seat cushions add a nautical splash of color to the seating area in the open pavilion.

right: Far away inland, in the far north of Sweden, a river frontage is utilized as a quiet spot to sit and dream in the evenings. At midsummer, the sun is still high until almost midnight.

far right: The smooth, bare rocks of the islands, called "skärgården" in Swedish, meaning "garden on the rocks," were worn smooth as the last ice age retreated.

alfresco eating

Eating outside is the perfect way to make the most of the summer, and a table and chairs can be set up in a sunny spot whether you have a large garden or just a tiny balcony. Your choice of outdoor furniture will depend on the space you have, but select from a hardwood, such as teak, or painted metals like wrought iron or steel, or cast aluminum.

Teak is a durable hardwood which, if left to weather naturally, will take on a pale, silvery gray colour, but its natural color can be sustained with a coat of oil twice a year. Be aware that a cloth used for oil can spontaneously combust, so leave it in a bucket of water afterward. Make sure, too, that any furniture comes from sustainable forests—the best sources are those owned and run by government agencies.

below left: Food always tastes better eaten in the open air, and a simple lunch of bread, cheese, and salad will make a quick break in the middle of the day feel like a feast.

below: If you have a large enough terrace or patio, what better way to entertain friends than to lay a long wooden table with plates and have a glass of wine and a shared meal.

right: Low-maintenance metal furniture is a good choice for smaller pieces of garden furniture and is easy to fold up and put away for the winter.

windowsill gardening

If you live in the city, and have no more than a bright and sunny window ledge, there's no reason why you can't still enjoy the delights of gardening and a taste of the outdoors. A window box or an array of pots along the sill can be nurtured and encouraged to grow many different varieties of plants, from zonal geraniums to cactus.

It's possible to grow an extensive range of vegetables and salads, too. Look for dwarf, compact, or early varieties as they crop earlier and usually need less space than taller types. Those listed in the seed catalogs as "baby" vegetables are particularly suitable. Chilli peppers, peas, beans and tomatoes, as well as short-rooted radishes, will crop well in a limited space, and some vegetable plants, including trailing species, are suitable for growing in hanging baskets fitted with integral drip trays. If you are intending to use heavy containers, put them on the floor just inside the window and support beans, peas, or tomatoes with twiggy sticks or bamboo canes pushed firmly into the potting compost at the time they are sown.

For a sunny, south-facing windowsill, a mixture of herbs from your local garden center can be planted in a long planter in good-quality potting mix. Choose herbs that don't grow too wide or tall—chives, basil, parsley, or thyme are ideal. Water the newly-planted herbs sparingly, and feed once a month with an organic, seaweed-based fertilizer. A small herb garden can be brought indoors for the winter, and you'll be able to harvest the leaves as you need them.

above far left: Most succulents and cacti grow only for a few months of the year, so only need watering during periods of growth. It's important not to water them for the rest of the year.

above left: Sempervivums, with their fleshy rosettes, will thrive in a sunny spot in well-drained potting compost. Their sculptural shapes and delicate colours make them a plant well-worth having in a windowsill garden.

below far left: Zonal pelargoniums, better known as geraniums, are renowned for their showy flower heads in shades of white, pink, and red. Choose dwarf varieties and snip off the flower heads as they fade.

below left: A city window looks out onto a bare brick wall, but a row of bushy white geraniums attracts the eye and gives the room a taste of a garden.

painted woodwork

Surrounding most Scandinavian houses, a painted wooden fence marks

the boundary line. From a simple picket fence to the most extravagantly

shaped borders, the creativity and inventiveness of the local carpenters

is to be seen on a walk around any old town. Painted white or blue, the

design of the fences adds a fabulous variety of shapes and textures to

the wildness of the old gardens and the neatness of the colourful houses.

The seaside port of Vaxholm was originally a fishing village, but today the

little town, with its narrow streets bounded with painted houses of every

color, is a popular vacation resort.

below: A white-painted picket fence is bordered with a simple trellis design and marks the periphery of a first-floor balcony that overlooks the street.

right: In many of the older houses, intricate wooden detailing is attached to the outside of the house. The curves of this wooden relief are painted white, in contrast to the pale gray of the paneling behind.

below: One of the most ubiquitous fencing designs, this cross-bar pattern is seen everywhere in Scandinavia, both inside and outside.

below right: A seventeenth-century fisherman's cottage has been recently renovated, and shows all the hallmarks of the traditional craftsmanship with its overhanging roofline and decorative details.

left: A furled modern rope is
stored on a painted branch in
the time-honoured tradition of
this ancient fishing port, where
a much harder life was lived in
the past by the fishermen and
their families.

right: The old boat house is
painted in the traditional Falun
red typical of so many Swedish
country houses since the
seventeenth century. The paint
is made from a pigment mined
in Falun, a town two hours' drive
from Stockholm.

midnight sun

In the far northern latitudes of Scandinavia, the countries of Finland, Norway, Sweden, and Iceland all experience the natural phenomenon of a sun that hardly sets around the time of midsummer. In fair weather, the sun is visible for twenty-four hours and the days sink slowly into a glorious golden light that bathes the surrounding countryside in a warm glow. In areas a little further south, the sun dips below the horizon for an hour or two, appearing with the swift dawn before it has ever become properly dark. The extreme polarity of this summer solstice is the long, dark winters, when the sun hardly, if at all, appears during the day. These extremes explain many things about the Scandinavian's obsession with light.

As a scarce commodity for so much of the year, any gleam of sun needs to be carefully conserved and celebrated. The midsummer festival on June 21st is one of the biggest holidays of the year. In Finland, Norway, and Denmark, bonfires are lit by the lakesides, while in Sweden a traditional maypole is dressed with flowers and danced around in every community.

left: Wooden decking is built out over a river in northern Sweden, and makes the perfect place to witness the sun sinking for a short time behind the horizon. The water becomes a channel of gold as the last rays slowly disappear.

right: Reflected in the shimmering water, a yellow-painted house keeps watch on the riverbank at the end of a long midsummer day.

sources

Garden design
Joan Edlis Associates (London)
www.joanedlislandscape.co.uk

Helena Molund (Vaxholm, Sweden)
Helena.molund@telia.com

Furniture
Furniture by Allinwood (Sweden)
www.allinwood.se

Scumble Goosie (UK)
www.scumble-goosie.co.uk

Sasha Waddell Furniture
www.sashawaddell.co.uk

Swede Home (USA)
www.swedehomeantiques.com

Graham & Green
www.grahamandgreen.co.uk

Avolli (USA)
www.avolli.com

Swedish Interior Design (UK)
www.swedishinteriordesign.co.uk

Lloyd Loom of Spalding
www.lloydloom.com

Interior Design
Angel + Blume
www.angelandblume.com

Annelis Winter at Winter Design
annaliswinter@mac.com

Portfolio
++(21) 020 8940 2217

Architects
Brady and Mallalieu
020 8880 1544

Lighting
Cameron Peters
www.cameronpeters.co.uk

Fabrics
Sasha Waddell
www.sashawaddell.co.uk

Ian Mankin
www.ianmankin.com

Mulberry
www.mulberry.com

Wallpaper
Cole & Son
www.cole-and-son.com

Duro
www.durosweden.se

Accessories

Lexington Company
Bedroom and bathroom
www.lexingtoncompany.com

Ceannis
www.ceannis.com

Emmaus
www.emmaus.org.uk

Ikea
www.ikea.com

Mateus
www.mateus.se

Manon
www.manoninteriors.co.uk

Himla
www.himla.se

The English Stamp Company
www.englishstamp.com

Sandra Jane
www.sandrajane.co.uk

Trip Trap Oil (for wooden floors)

Wooden Flooring Sales
www.woodenflooringsales.com

Eva Johnson
www.evajohnson.co.uk

Flowers

The Flower House
www.theflowerhouse.co.uk

Wild Bunch
www.wildbunch.uk.com

Swedish tile stoves

Peter C. Moore Masonry Inc. (USA)
www.vtbrickoven.com

Lindholm Kakelugnar (Sweden)
www.lindholm-kakelugnar.com

Places to visit in Sweden

Skansen, in Stockholm
www.skansen.se

The home of Carl and Karin Larsson,
in Sundborn
www.carllarsson.se

Gripsholm Castle, in Mariefred
www.royalcourt.se

Nordic Museum, in Stockholm
www.nordiskamuseet.se

index

acknowledgments

I would like to thank the following for being so relaxed and gracious, for allowing us to photograph their beautiful houses and being so completely welcoming:
Annelis Winter, Christina and Per Durling, Mia and Hakan Nilson (and Mia's father, Soren Ericsson, who built the house), Annali Liljenfeld, Annis and Claes Anders.

With special thanks to Helena Molund who gave so unstintingly of her time and supplied flowers for the Vaxholm shoots, and to Per Molund who ferried us between islands on his boat—they both made us so welcome. Thanks, too, to Annike and Per Marklund who entertained us and were such great hosts. Also to Joan Edlis, Ann and Mick Brownfield, Jon and Sasha Dorey, Sasha Waddell, and Lis Drinkwater; and with special thanks to Jane Cassini for her brilliant styling. Also many thanks to Cate Burren, without whose enthusiasm at the beginning of the project I might never have started in the first place, and to my editor Gillian Haslam who encouraged and spurred me on and to Christine Wood for all her work in creating such beautiful pages. And many thanks to my publisher, Cindy Richards, for all her support and enthusiasm with this and other projects.

I would also like to thank the inimitable Mark Scott, whose company on the trips was as entertaining and sparky as ever, and whose magical photography turned all my ideas into something completely special.